Sol Search: A Journey Through

SPAIN

Diary of a Traveling Black Woman: A Guide to International Travel

Mini Travel Guide Series

Dubai, Abu Dhabi & The 5 Other Emirates You Didn't Know About

Jamaica: Likkle, but Tallawah!

Studying Abroad for Black Women

Iceland: Nature, Nurture, & Adventure

Solo Travel: Try It At Least Once!

Taiwan: An Underrated Paradise

And more...

Diary of a Traveling Black Woman:
A Guide to International Travel

"Mini Travel Guide Series"
Volume XIII - Spain

Sol Search:
A Journey Through Spain

Kamryn Kinlow

The Traveling Black Women Network
Grace Royal International, LLC
Atlanta, GA

Cover Model: Kamryn Kinlow
Cover Design: Nadine C. Duncan
Interior Design: Nadine C. Duncan

ISBN: 979-8-9889182-5-7
ISBN: 979-8-218-64752-0 (eBook)

1st Edition, September 2025
Travel Guide Series, Volume XIII
Printed in the United States of America

Published in the United States by:
Traveling Black Women™
Grace Royal International, LLC
Atlanta, GA 30316

www.travelingblackwomen.com

To my mom,

You aren't here in the physical, so I carry you
through spirit. Though our time together was brief,
I feel your presence in every step I take and
every moment of beauty I witness. You will always
live through me, and everything I do is a reflection
of the love and strength you gave me.

From your one and only daughter...
this is for you.

Contents

At first traveling leaves you speechless, and then it turns you into a storyteller...

Preface

Reflection (2025)

Rereading my journal, I find power in knowing that my thoughts & my ideas, became real. Sometimes, God gives you the thought, but not the plan. That's the beautiful thing about life, watching it unfold.

The process really is the reward...

From Ink to Existence...

June 21, 2021

It's time to pack up and start focusing on me—the things I truly want. I'm ready to travel.

November 8, 2021

Teach in a foreign country. Find places where vaccinations won't be overwhelming.

January 1, 2022

Travel with others and alone. Get that passport.

June 1, 2023

Curate a book.

"Write down a revelation and make it clear so that a herald may run with it. The revelation is for an appointed time; it speaks of the end and will not prove false. Though it lingers, wait for it; it will certainly come and will not delay."

— Habakkuk 2:2-3

Going Abroad

I've always dreamed of moving abroad. Since college days. I am proof that a thought can translate into reality. Life has shown me that the perfectly crafted timeline does not always reflect a personal timeline. Here's a look into my not so perfect timeline...

Alexa, play "Lost" by Frank Ocean

...

Let's backtrack to 2019...

I made the decision to complete my Associate's degree at Berkeley College in December 2019 with a plan to transfer to a school that offered study abroad options. It was a tough choice because I had everything I thought I needed. I was living right outside of New York City in White Plains, New York just 20 minutes from the city. I had friends who felt like family, I was close to my own family, and I had a job.

I was comfortable.

Deep down, the only thing I felt truly drawn to was traveling, even though I couldn't explain why. It was just something that felt natural to me. So, I applied to the University at Albany in upstate New York because they offered so many study abroad opportunities.

I'll never forget checking my email during a shift at my internship at White Plains Hospital and reading my acceptance letter.

I wasn't thrilled about moving to upstate New York in the middle of winter, but the chance to attend a university and the opportunities that came with it made the move exciting.

January 2020...

I don't think I was even on campus for a week before I went in search of the study abroad office. At the time, I was studying Healthcare and discovered a Healthcare Research program in Italy, an experiential learning opportunity that immediately caught my attention.

To apply, I had to write an essay for the "Bridge the Gap" Scholarship, which would help cover the cost of the program. Growing up with only my father, paying for programs like this was a huge financial burden. I needed to take advantage of every resource available and make the right connections to make it happen.

Reading back that 'Bridge the Gap' scholarship essay, I'm so proud of the 19-year-old me who knew what she wanted, even though she didn't fully understand the incredible opportunities that were about to come her way in the travel world. I realize now that that version of myself has grown to be even more passionate, curious and thoughtful about the world. I am proud to say I always knew the impact I brought to the world as a Black woman.

Here's a part of that scholarship essay from my younger self:

Underrepresentation is a part of my story. As a first-generation student facing financial hardships, the path has never been easy. Opportunities to gain knowledge and travel abroad are rare in the community I come from. That's why I'm striving to bring those opportunities back to my community. I haven't had the chance to travel outside the United States, but I've always known there's so much more the world has to offer. Studying abroad, for me, is a chance to break the cycles that often define minority communities by sharing the lessons I've learned abroad. I often ask myself these questions:

- What experiences can I gain from going outside of my community?
- What lessons can I bring back to my community for growth?
- How will studying abroad allow me to be the change in my community?

I am a firm believer that a change starts from within. If I want to be the change, I have to start somewhere.

This moment is where my journey begins...

Or, so I thought…

I had been accepted into the Italy program, and I was beyond excited. But then, due to the COVID-19 status, travel in and out of Italy was halted. The study abroad department recommended applying to a program in another country, so I chose Nairobi, Kenya. It had nothing to do with my degree program, but my hunger to travel was undeniable. I was willing to go anywhere.

Then, just as quickly as things had started, everything came to a screeching halt. In March, as we were preparing for spring break, the reality of the COVID-19 pandemic set in. I remember receiving a protocol update telling us to pack what we could because there was a real chance we wouldn't be returning to campus soon. My plans, my dreams of studying abroad, were suddenly dashed.

Alexa play,
"Things will get better"
by Cleo Sol

During the pandemic, life felt like a filler episode–

leaving college to move back home, locked up like Repunzel for months… social distancing, masking, finishing school online, transitioning back to work… You all know, you were there. The mundane. A life lived for work, not working to live. Boring.

For a while, life felt stagnant. It didn't seem like anything was going back to normal. I was 19 when COVID forced me to pause my college experience. I didn't return to campus for classes until my senior year, in 2022.

But life had changed.

I had gone from living in a dorm to managing an apartment, taking care of a car note, and balancing a full-time job while being a full-time student. I was suddenly catapulted into adulthood with no transition.

I got caught up in the grind of it all and started to resent the cycle of daily responsibilities. I had come to Albany with the sole goal of studying abroad, not to get caught up in the weight of adult life. But… If the pandemic gave me anything, it was time to think. So, I started looking into programs again.

I applied to teach English in Japan—a highly competitive program with an intense application process. I wasn't accepted. Then, I tried again in 2023, only to be denied once more.

After finishing school in 2022, I found myself stuck in a job I didn't love. One particularly bad day at work pushed me to start researching again.

I saved up some extra money from working overtime during the summer of 2023, so I decided to apply for a teaching program in Madrid, Spain through CIEE. Unfortunately, I was waitlisted and eventually told there were no more spots available.

However, a helpful advisor suggested I apply for the volunteer program. It required working three days a week and living with a host family who provided meals in exchange for English conversation practice.

Oh, and I would be living in a small village...

Honestly, this was not exactly the idea I had in mind for myself. At this point, I want to say the cliche thing, "It was the perfect opportunity!" but nope. I did not even think that at all... Not even a little bit.

I was not ready to go from living on my own to living with a family I knew nothing about, to translating everything, and all the things that come along with that transition. But... you can't always believe your thoughts. So, I went in with the mindset of 'I'll try it. And, worst case scenario if I hate it there, I'll come back home...'

So... I joined CIEE's Volunteer Program in Spain and

after paying the application fee, it was just a waiting game until I got my placement.

I didn't have much time to mentally prepare for the experience, as I was informed of my placement super late. They told me to hold off on booking my flight until everything was confirmed, so I waited…and waited.

Finally, about two weeks before heading to Spain, I got the news. I was placed in a village called **Cuéllar** at a bilingual school called CIEP Santa Clara which served students from kindergarten to fourth grade. Each class had assigned teachers who spoke English as a second language, but my role was to be the native speaker—spending 30 minutes a week with each classroom, essentially teaching the entire school.

Along with my school placement, I received the contact information for my host family. I was going to live with my host mom, her partner, and their two young children, ages 7 and 5.

I reached out to get a feel for the family, and we FaceTimed as they sent pictures of where I'd be staying. I was excited, though a bit nervous since my Spanish skills weren't the best. Still, I was ready for the adventure ahead.

After a 4 year journey,
I finally arrived in Spain on April 8, 2024

The Castilla y León region where I lived has deep roots in Spanish history. It was one of the first areas in Spain to be reclaimed from the Moors during the Reconquista, a period when Christian kingdoms gradually recaptured territory from Muslim rule. The Kingdom of Castile, which makes up part of modern-day Castilla y León, was instrumental in this effort, and as the region grew in power, so did the language spoken there **Castilian.**

The development of Castilian, or what we now call Spanish, is largely attributed to the region. The earliest known written texts in Castilian come from here, and over time, this dialect became the foundation for modern Spanish. By the time of the reign of the Catholic Monarchs, Castilian had emerged as the dominant language of the Iberian Peninsula, largely due to the influence of the Kingdom of Castile.

The region played a critical role in shaping Spain's identity and is a must-see for anyone interested in medieval history, language, and culture.

"Protect my next steps as I move to Spain, allow this transition to come with ease..."

What to Know

Trip Preparation

Getting There

I had to be in Spain by April 8 for program orientation and pick-up. Of course, I left everything to the last minute (because why not?), but I made it.

I flew out of Newark Liberty Airport on April 7, 2024, on a red-eye. I had seven hours to think about what I had done. Did I really pack my stuff up and fly across the Atlantic? The entire time I thought to myself, this is probably the craziest thing I've ever done.

I landed in Spain the next morning, tired but hyped. Honestly, I never felt scared, just more so concerned about whether or not this would actually work out, you know?

My one-way ticket set me back about $650 with United Airlines, and I shelled out $21 for in-flight WiFi. That $21 was definitely worth it for keeping my sanity during the flight. I had my shows and could doom scroll through Tiktok, so I was fine!

Visa Situation—Smooth Sailing

Thankfully, there was no visa drama for me since I was

on a short-term program. The main reason I signed up for this program was because they handled all the essentials. I was able to stay in Spain for up to 90 days as a tourist based on the Schengen Zone rules.

The Schengen Zone rules allow you to bounce around most of Europe for three months without hassle. Just keep an eye on your days. No one wants to get banned from the European Union.

Here's the tea with the Schengen Zone:

It's a group of 27 European countries that agreed to let people travel freely across their borders without needing to show a passport or go through border checks. It's like moving between states back in the US. Easy and seamless.

For Americans, this means you can stay in this zone for up to 90 days within a 180-day period without a visa.

But there's a catch... Once you hit those 90 days, you have to leave, and you can't come back until another 90 days have passed.

If you leave the Schengen Zone before reaching the 90-day limit, the clock stops on your 90-day count. When you return, the days you've already spent in the zone still count toward your total, so you can only stay for the remaining days out of the original 90-day allowance.

The 180-day period is always rolling, meaning you should keep track of your time spent in the zone to avoid overstaying.

Vaccinations

No vaccinations required, thank goodness. Needles? No, thank you. I wasn't interested in getting a bunch of shots, so Europe was the perfect option for me. I'm all for holistic remedies: oil of oregano, vitamin C, iron supplements, and staying hydrated. These keep my immune system in check, especially when I'm far from home.

Pharmacy Adventures

Visiting the pharmacies here was a real eye-opener! I didn't expect Spanish pharmacies to be so different from what I'm used to.

For starters, some medications you need a prescription for in the U.S. are available over-the-counter here. It's kinda wild to think how accessible that makes things.

But the real gem is how pharmacies here are more like community health centers. The pharmacists aren't just filling prescriptions. They're giving medical advice,

doing health screenings, and even minor treatments. It's such a different vibe from the more transactional experience I was used to.

Also, the range of products is impressive. I found so many cool skincare items and natural remedies that you just don't see in U.S. pharmacies. They also have extended hours, and some are even open 24/7. It's like they really get that people need access to health resources at all times.

All in all, these pharmacies feel like a community hub where people get a personal touch and genuine help. It's refreshing and kind of inspiring to see how different it can be.

Packing

Packing was a whole other adventure. Here's how I handled it (Like a G I must say)!

Hair Care:

Bring it all!

If you're anything like me, you're going to want to pack ALL your serums, deep conditioners, shampoos, heat protectants... basically, anything hair-related, make sure you have it before you land in Spain.

Sure, you can find some products in places like **La Latina in Madrid**, which has all the beauty supply stores, but if you're heading to smaller regions like Castilla y León… good luck! You're not going to find them as easily, and ordering online is not the move when most of the good stuff can only be shipped within the U.S. Oh, and you might want to throw in a protective style.

Learn from my struggle.
Come prepared.

Shoes:

Forget the heels. You won't wear them. If you aren't going to wear it for anything but fashion, I repeat leave it at home! What you do need are some *solid walking shoes*. I'm talking about Saucony, New Balance, Nike, anything comfy that won't have you regretting life decisions after walking all day. And, don't forget your insoles!

If you do want to wear a dressy heel, go for a platform or something with a chunky heel. Stilettos aren't really the style. Most people opt for strappy platform sandals, heeled espadrilles, or similar comfortable yet stylish options.

Your feet will thank you later!

Clothes:

Where do I even start? The weather in Castilla y León is wildly unpredictable. I showed up in April thinking, "Oh, it's going to be warm and sunny." **WRONG!** I was rocking sweaters and coats all the way until June. The mornings are freezing, the afternoons are scorching, and the nights are back to being cold.

Do yourself a favor and pack for every season. It's like weather roulette out here! And if you're like me, fashion-forward but also practical, don't stress about overpacking too much because you're going to end up shopping anyway (and isn't shopping abroad kind of the point?). Plus, you might as well use Global Blue for that tax-free perk!

Global Blue Tax-Free Shopping allows U.S. residents (and other non-EU tourists) to get a refund on the VAT (Value Added Tax) they paid on goods purchased in European Union countries.

Here's how it works in simple terms:

Shop:
Buy items from stores that offer tax-free shopping (look for the Global Blue or Tax-Free Shopping sign).

Ask:
When you make a purchase, ask the store for a **tax**

refund form. They will give you a document to fill out, which includes your details and a receipt.

Get Stamp:
When you're about to leave the EU, present your tax refund form, receipts, and the purchased goods to customs at the airport or border. They'll stamp your form to confirm you're exporting the goods.

Claim Refund:
After getting the stamp, return the form to a Global Blue desk or mail it to the address provided. You can then choose to receive your refund as cash, credit card credit, or bank transfer.

...

Nutrition & Health:

Spain's food is absolutely incredible! Vibrant, flavorful, and rich with history. Many of the popular foods in Spain weren't what I was used to eating when I first arrived. They are very big on ham, salami, and other cured meats, but I don't eat pork. However, here's a little secret just for my readers... I cheated every now and then. And honestly? It was AMAZING. Sometimes, I just couldn't resist.

The Spanish style of eating is also very different from what I was used to. If you're accustomed to meals with one meat, one starch, and a vegetable, get ready for a change.

Spanish meals are usually large and more family-style. Specifically, living with my host family, we'd always have a fresh baguette cut up to eat with every meal, along with some fresh-cut fruit, olives, cheese, and maybe some type of fish like salmon. Sometimes, the main dish would be something like eggplant lasagna. Instead of individual plates with set portions, meals were set up so that everyone could pick a little bit of everything. It felt more communal, and honestly, I grew to love it.

Spain also has something called Spanish tortilla, a simple yet beloved dish made of eggs and potatoes. It's a national favorite—everyone there loves it.

And while most people associate Spain with sangria, I quickly realized that the real local favorite is beer—specifically, a cerveza con limón (beer with lemon). The olives were fresh and delicious, and the seafood? Incredibly fresh.

Spain introduced me to a whole new side of myself. A pork eater… a beer drinker… who would've thought?

But let me tell you, if your stomach decides to act brand new (which it probably will), you're going to need some survival tools. The Mediterranean diet is healthy, but your system might need time to adjust to all the new flavors and spices. My top tip?

Always have these on hand:
- Oil of Oregano
- Vitamin C
- Activated Charcoal

These became my lifesavers when my stomach decided it wasn't quite ready for the Spanish feast. Oil of oregano is great for gut health, Vitamin C keeps your immune system in check, and activated charcoal can help with any, uh, unexpected digestive issues. Trust me, they're worth packing!

Iron and B12 are also a must. Spanish culture is incredibly active, and keeping your energy up is key. From exploring the winding streets of historic cities to late-night socializing, you'll want to stay energized for all that Spain has to offer.

Miscellaneous Must-Haves:

Now, this might sound a little extra, but pack some washcloths and hand soap. You'd be surprised how many places don't have hand soap readily available. No joke, you'll be thanking yourself when you're out and about. Before going to Europe, really think about the conveniences you have in the United States. Take a moment to analyze the little things you love—your favorite hand soap, toilet tissue, washcloths, bath soap, mouthwash, and face cream. Make sure to stock up on all of that because, in the small village where I lived, the only brands I could find were big commercial ones. My natural soap, washcloths, lotion—all of that was nowhere to be found.

Alexa,
Play "Blessed" by Wizkid

What to Expect

My Typical Workday

My typical workday looked like this: My schedule was usually from 7 a.m. to 1 p.m., Monday to Thursday, although some days were shorter. During the school day, I taught one class for 45 minutes, then moved on to the next. I worked with different classes each week, which gave me a chance to teach a variety of age groups and experience different lesson plans. The teachers were very supportive and gave me the freedom to design my own lessons. They also stepped in to help with classroom management when needed.

I'm *more* Than

A basketball player because I'm going to be famous also teacher, doctor and artist because they are going to be so funny and practiced ingles

The students were really interested in me being from New York, and that made teaching so much fun. A lot of my lessons centered around New York—its landmarks, food, hip hop, and fashion. I loved sharing pieces of my culture with them. Sometimes, I'd expand the lessons to talk about the U.S. as a whole, which turned out to be a bit more challenging than I expected. There are so many cultural differences across the country,

from New York to California, but it made the experience all the more rewarding.

After school, I helped my host siblings with their English homework or engaged with them through play. We'd draw pictures, play games, or play soccer outside, all in English. The goal was to make learning fun while helping them build their conversational English skills.

On Thursdays, I tutored a local woman in Cuéllar, an English teacher herself, in conversational English. Our lessons were more relaxed, taking the form of a walk where we'd speak for 30 minutes in English and 30 minutes in Spanish. It was a great way for me to practice my Spanish, and over time, we became really close.

An Active Lifestyle

One of the biggest adjustments for me was how active everyone was. I'm talking about walking everywhere. Public transport is great, but if you can walk, you walk. Whether it's running errands or meeting friends, walking is the default mode of transportation. I noticed it wasn't just adults either. The kids are super active too. It was refreshing to see children actually playing outside, and not glued to phones or tablets.

Living in Spain taught me a lot about getting outside. In the U.S., it's so easy to stay home—your couch, Netflix, maybe some takeout. But in Spain, especially in my little village of Cuéllar, life just happened outdoors. People didn't need an excuse to be out; they'd just gather in the plaza, stroll around, or chat with neighbors like it was second nature.

Cuéllar was full of hills. And when I say hills, I mean serious, calf-burning inclines that I faced every day. Just walking around, I stayed toned without even trying. I'd be huffing and puffing up those slopes, while the locals, including my host family, just cruised along, unfazed, like they'd been doing it forever (which they probably had).

Then there were my host kids, who kept me moving more than anything else. They loved playing soccer, and I'd join them on our patio almost daily. They had all the tricks, teaching me moves and giggling every time I missed the ball or stumbled trying to keep up. For them, it wasn't exercise; it was just fun. Playtime, family time, all rolled into one.

Back home, it's so easy to settle indoors, but in Spain, life was meant to be lived in the open air. That mindset shift was one of the most refreshing parts of my time there.

My host mom was part of a run club that met on Wednesdays, which inspired me to get moving, and my host siblings were in every sport imaginable. I saw kids rollerblading, running, and what really blew my mind was how many of them were into triathlons. It was incredible to witness their energy and athleticism. Being surrounded by such an active community definitely pushed me to get out there more and embrace that lifestyle.

Cultural Norms

I truly admire Black women who step into new environments and unapologetically take up space, myself included. We have an incredible ability to adapt to different cultural norms while still showing up as our full, authentic selves. It's a testament to our strength and resilience that no matter where we go, we find ways to thrive and make an impact.

Let's dive into the cultural side of things...

Spain has its own rhythm, and Castilla y León is no different. Here are some things I noticed:

Socializing:

This was a big one for me. Coming from New York, where the culture is super individualistic (think everyone minding their own business, headphones in, rushing from one place to another). Spain felt like a different world. In the small village where I lived, everything revolves around community. People take the time to greet each other, chat with their neighbors, and actually enjoy spending time together. It's not just about existing side by side; it's about building relationships.

I had to remind myself to slow down and engage with people in a way that felt really foreign at first, but in the best way possible.

Spanish Kisses:

If you're not an affectionate person or you're opposed to physical touch, get ready for an adjustment. The dos besos, **the double cheek kiss**, is the standard greeting, even if you've just met someone. It's a sign of warmth and openness, but if you're used to keeping your personal space bubble intact, this might be a bit challenging at first. But over time, I found it's just another way to feel connected to the people around you.

Siesta:

This was hands down my favorite norm to adjust to. Imagine this: it's the middle of the day, and instead of pushing through that afternoon slump, everything just shuts down. Stores close, streets get quiet, and everyone takes a break. It's like the world hits pause, giving you permission to relax, recharge, and then jump back into your day with fresh energy.

I honestly don't know why we don't do this in the United States. In Spain, the entire rhythm of the day revolves around it. Schools let out around 1 p.m., and parents or family members pick up the kids to bring them home for lunch. Lunch isn't a quick bite, it's a full meal, often lasting until 3 p.m. After that, adults return to work to finish the day, and life picks back up in the evening.

Organized Day:

The structure of the day in Spain was something I quickly came to appreciate. Your day isn't just about work; it's about balance. Mornings start with a break for coffee with coworkers, which felt more like a mini social event than a quick caffeine fix. Lunch, which is the biggest meal of the day, is usually enjoyed at home and often followed by a siesta.

Afterward, you return to work or your afternoon activities and then have dinner much later in the evening. This slower pace, especially compared to the nonstop grind in New York, was refreshing. Plus, the fact that lunch is the main meal means you really get to savor it. Good conversation, and no rush to get back to your desk.

Living with a Host Family

One of the most transformative parts of my time in Spain was living with a host family. Before arriving, I didn't know what to expect. How would I adjust to a new home, in a new culture, with people I'd never met? But looking back, I realize it was one of the most valuable experiences of my time abroad.

My host family in Castilla y León lived a very busy life, which was hard for me to keep up with, especially in those first couple of weeks. Coming from a more independent lifestyle in New York, I wasn't used to constantly being around people, and suddenly, I found myself in a home where there was always something happening.

I had to get used to socializing all the time, something that pushed me way out of my comfort zone. People were constantly expecting me to talk, engage, and connect, which was such a change from what I was used to. It was a challenge, but also something that helped me grow.

We ate lunch and dinner together every night. I sat right across from my host mom at the dinner table and next to my host brother. We would set the table for dinner together and clean up as a family. After my host parents put the kids to bed, they would come back downstairs, and we'd all settle in to watch Buscando Amor, a Spanish reality dating show. I love reality TV, no matter what language it's in, so I was hooked. I'd read the subtitles in English while picking up on the Spanish dialogue.

Sometimes, we'd switch things up and watch Bridgerton. My host parents always offered to change it to English for me, but I insisted on watching in Spanish.

It was one of the best ways to improve my language skills without even realizing it.

Looking back, I cherish those moments so much because this wasn't something I grew up doing. I was used to meals being quick and on the go, but here, we sat down as a family every day, sharing stories, laughing, and learning from one another. It gave me a deeper sense of connection to the family and to Spanish culture.

Moving in with a host family in Spain was packed with firsts for me. For one, it was the first time I'd ever lived in a house—like, a real house, and this was no regular place. It was huge, super modern, and smack in the middle of this historic village, which was extremely trippy. The house even had an elevator! We had a woman who came by to handle laundry every day, my sheets were freshly washed each week, and there was even an in-home gym. I honestly felt like I was living in an episode of The Fresh Prince of Bel-Air.

But beyond all the luxurious adjustments, there were other, more personal firsts. This was also the first time I'd lived with a woman in the household—a "mom," in a way. Growing up, I'd only lived with my dad, who worked constantly, and while I do have siblings, we weren't raised together. Yes, I've got a huge family, but I'd never experienced that close-knit, "traditional" family life you see on TV.

Living with my host family was a whole new dynamic, and it changed something in me. I know it sounds deep, but this experience was life-changing in ways that I don't think many people would fully understand. Moving to Europe would've been amazing on its own, but getting to be part of a family like this really shifted something in my brain chemistry.

I'm honestly convinced God crafted this experience for me. Not because it was what I thought I wanted, but because it was exactly what I needed.

Balancing family life with my desire to explore Spain wasn't always easy. There were times when I had to make tough decisions...

Should I miss a birthday party to book this cheap flight to another city?

Most of the time, I chose traveling because I wanted to see as much as I could while I was there.

I also made it a priority to spend time with my host family. I wanted to make the most of the relationships I was building, especially since it was through them that I got to know locals. One of my host mom's friends became very close with me. We would take walks together every Sunday, and it was one of those simple but special connections that added depth to my experience.

Of course, living in someone else's home came with its challenges. There were definitely times when I felt some tension. Whether it was due to cultural differences or the language barrier, communication wasn't always smooth.

Spain's culture can be quite passive, which was a big adjustment for me coming from New York where people are more direct. If someone had an issue with me, they wouldn't always say it outright. That was strange to me, but it taught me to be more observant and mindful of subtle social cues.

Living with a host family also meant following their rules. I couldn't just come and go as I pleased, like I was used to back in New York. There were routines to follow, expectations to meet, and that took some adjusting.

I had to let go of the freedom I was so accustomed to and embrace this new, more structured way of life. It wasn't always easy, but in the end, I came to appreciate the experience. It taught me how to be flexible, respectful, and considerate in a new environment.

Despite the challenges, living with a host family gave me something priceless—a deep, authentic connection to Spanish culture that I wouldn't have gotten any other way.

It was an experience that pushed me to grow in ways I hadn't anticipated and left me with lasting memories that I'll always carry with me.

Getting Around

Navigating Castilla y León is a unique experience, especially if you're used to the hustle and bustle of cities like New York.

Here's how you can get around:

Buses:

Getting around Castilla y León is all about the buses. I was a little skeptical at first, but they're actually pretty reliable. They connect all the little towns and cities, which is great when you're trying to explore on a budget. I'd tell my New York self that it's like taking a Greyhound, but the scenery is way better and, surprisingly, more chill. Just don't expect the same frequency as an MTA city bus. You'll actually have to plan your trips out here.

Intercity Buses:

Okay, so the intercity buses are a game-changer. These buses connect major spots like Valladolid, León, Burgos, and Salamanca to all the smaller, more rural areas. It's like the Megabus but with fewer college kids and more scenic views. It's wild how quickly you can get from one historic city to another, all while sitting comfortably with your headphones in, pretending you're in a European indie movie.

Trains:

Let's talk trains. My favorite mode of transport in Spain. Castilla y León is super connected by train, thanks to Renfe and the AVE. You can take a train from Valladolid and be in Madrid before you finish your playlist.

These trains were a completely different vibe than what I was used to. Way calmer. No chaos, no over-policing and no rats. It's more laid-back, and the seats are more comfortable. Plus, you get to see the Spanish countryside while traveling. It's a little reminder that even though I'm far from home, I can still get places fast.

Walking:

Oh, the walking. My New York self thought I knew what walking was all about, but Castilla y León streets taught me something new. The streets here are historic, narrow, and so charming that you'll forget how long you've been walking. It's less about dodging people and more about soaking in the atmosphere. Walking was the best way to stumble upon the cutest cafes, bars and hidden spots in my village, as well as get to know the area a bit more.

BlaBlaCar:

Okay, I'll admit... BlaBlaCar was a bit of a leap for me. Carpooling with strangers? Not a thing for me back home. But it's a legit way to get around here, especially if you're trying to save some euros and meet new people. It's kind of like UberPool but on a whole other level. And, honestly, it's kind of fun.

I'm usually quiet in the car, but there's something cool about sharing a ride with someone who's from a completely different part of the world. I met a lot of interesting people using BlaBlaCar, though the experience could be a bit hit-or-miss.

Some drivers were super reliable, while others didn't always confirm the ride. It's definitely a convenient way to get from point A to point B, but it can be challenging if you don't know much Spanish, as most of the drivers I met spoke limited English.

Flights:

Lastly, flights. So, the train is amazing for getting around Spain, but when you need to go further, Madrid-Barajas is your go-to. It's like my JFK or LaGuardia—but in Spain. Whether you're catching a flight back to New York (if you're feeling homesick) or hopping over to another European country, Madrid is the hub.

Even though it's a major airport, it somehow feels less chaotic than JFK during the holiday season.

Honorable mention goes to the Valladolid Airport, located in the Castilla y León area! It might not have the widest range of destinations, but it does fly to some nice spots:

- Barcelona (Ryanair),
- Gran Canaria (Las Palmas) with Binter Canarias
- Ibiza (Iberia)
- Palma de Mallorca (Iberia/Ryanair)
- Tenerife (Iberia)
- Valencia (Iberia).

Pros & Cons for Black Women

Alexa,
Play "Special" By Lizzo ft SZA

Cons

Cultural Differences in Social Norms

Okay, so let's be real. The culture shock is undeniable when you're a Black woman in Spain, especially in smaller towns. People often have a narrow view of what a Black woman "should" be like, based mostly on what they've seen on TV or online. That means they might expect you to fit into a box that doesn't reflect who you really are. It can be frustrating, feeling like you're constantly being seen through a lens of stereotypes.

But this experience also made me reflect in a deeper way. I still wonder if Black women will ever be fully seen for all that we are. The reality is, people often form opinions about us before we even speak—no matter how we present ourselves.

Being in Spain, I had moments where I thought, "If I'm not fully seen in my own country, can I really expect to be seen here?" It's a tough question, and it made me realize that this challenge exists no matter where we go.

But here's the thing: despite those preconceived notions, despite the ways we might be undervalued or misunderstood, we're still here. We're still taking up space in places people never expected to see us, and we're doing things they thought we couldn't.

That's powerful...

Every step we take, every achievement, is proof that we belong, even in spaces that weren't designed for us. So even if the world isn't always ready to see us, that doesn't stop us from being seen.

Steady Stares / Extreme Curiosity

If you think you're gonna blend in, think again. Especially in those smaller towns, people will look at you like you're some kind of exotic bird. The stares can be intense and constant because you might be the only Black person they've seen in a while...or ever. It's not necessarily hostile, but it does get awkward when you're just trying to go about your day.

Along with the constant staring, people weren't shy about addressing me directly in the street. I often heard *morena*, meaning "brown," and sometimes *negrita*, meaning "little Black girl." While morena was more neutral, negrita could feel off-putting, depending on the tone and intent. These terms reflected the way locals categorized me at a glance, sometimes out of curiosity, other times with a sense of familiarity that I didn't always welcome.

Language Barrier

Let me tell you, the Spanish I thought I knew went right out the window when I got there. The dialect in Spain, particularly in regions like Castilla y León, is fast, like rapid-fire fast. And don't even get me started on the different pronunciations and accents. It's wild how the language varies so much depending on where you are. In places like Segovia or Cuéllar, I noticed a lot of people speaking with a lisp— completely threw me off.

Awkwardness Around Identity

Most of the awkwardness from Spaniards could usually be cleared up with a simple conversation and a bit of education. Many people just hadn't encountered a Black American before and genuinely didn't understand the distinction between being Black and being African. It was frustrating, but it often came from ignorance rather than malice.

But when it came to other Black people throughout the diaspora, those from France, Africa, London, people who knew their direct lineage, I found that I dealt with the most ignorance around identity from them. It was interesting, and at times saddening, to hear other Black people's thoughts on Black Americans.

There was this idea that because we don't always know our exact lineage, we have no culture, no roots. Some believed that being Black in America was a watered-down experience, as if our history, struggles, and contributions weren't enough to form a real identity.

It was ironic... Here I was, experiencing culture shock in Spain, yet some of the deepest discomfort around my identity didn't come from Spaniards at all, but from other Black people who viewed Blackness through the lens of nationality and ancestry in ways that excluded me.

What made it even more disheartening was seeing just how much White propaganda has been pushed to the point where Black Americans aren't even considered part of American history when in reality, we are the history. The very foundation of America was built on the backs of Black people. Our culture, our resilience, our impact is woven into every part of the country, yet so many people, even within the diaspora, have absorbed the idea that we are somehow separate, as if we exist outside of the narrative rather than being central to it.

And the irony? The world consumes Black American

culture in mass. Our music, our fashion, our slang, our style—it's everywhere. People around the world imitate the way we talk, the way we move, the way we express ourselves.

Hip-hop, which started as an expression of Black struggle and resilience in the Bronx, is now one of the biggest cultural exports in the world. Our influence is undeniable. Yet somehow, despite this global consumption, we still find ourselves having to defend our culture's existence.

At times, it felt like I had to prove that being a Black American was just as valid, that our culture—built from survival, resistance, and creativity—wasn't something to dismiss. But it was also a reminder of the lasting effects of colonialism and displacement, and how the fractures within the diaspora still shape the way we see one another.

Pros

Cultural Exchange

One of the coolest things about being a Black woman in Spain? You get to flip the script and educate others on what it really means to be a Black American. Trust me, you'll have plenty of chances to share your experiences and break down those stereotypes.

While teaching, I made it a point to educate my students on Black culture, Black icons, and the diversity within the Black community. I explained things like the different shades of skin color among Black people and how, in America, Black individuals come from all over the world, representing a rich tapestry of backgrounds and histories.

Many of my activities focused on exposure; I had them read books featuring diverse representation and watch short films that highlighted Black culture. It was rewarding to bridge those cultural gaps and watch their curiosity grow, deepening their understanding of different cultures while allowing me to celebrate my identity in a new way. It's kind of empowering to know that you're changing perceptions just by being you.

Welcoming Atmosphere

I've gotta say, the vibe in Spain is on point. The people are warm, friendly, and genuinely interested in getting to know you. You'll feel welcomed, which can make the whole experience so much smoother. It's nice to be in a place where people are open to new faces and different cultures.

I remember my first day of class during introductions when I casually mentioned that I loved dessert (that's the foodie in me!). To my surprise, the students literally started pulling treats out of their bags to share with me. It was such a sweet gesture and perfectly illustrated their warm and generous spirit.

Travel Opportunities

Now, this is where it gets exciting. Spain is a gateway to so many incredible places with rich African heritage. Whether you're hopping over to Morocco or exploring other parts of Europe, traveling is easy and affordable. It's like the whole continent is at your fingertips, and you can dive into the history and culture of the African diaspora in ways that just aren't possible in the U.S.

Connection with the Diaspora

If you find yourself in cities like Barcelona or Madrid, you're in for a treat. These places are like melting pots, where you can connect with people from all over. Africa, the Caribbean, you name it. It's an amazing opportunity to bond with a broader diaspora and feel that sense of community, even when you're far from home.

Navigating Connection as a Black Woman in Spain

During my time living in Spain, meeting people as a Black woman was an eye-opening experience, both enriching and challenging. While I encountered warm, genuine connections, there were moments where I felt like my race became the focal point of interactions in ways that were uncomfortable and, at times, alienating.

Fetishization and Being "Exotic"

One of the most striking aspects of connecting in Spain was the fetishization I experienced. Spain, like many European countries, doesn't have a large Black population in most regions, so being a Black woman often meant standing out in a crowd.

Unfortunately, this novelty sometimes turned into fetishization. I found myself reduced to an "exotic" curiosity, with some men openly admitting they had never dated or even interacted with a Black woman before. The fascination wasn't with who I was as a person, but rather the novelty of my appearance.

I was often met with assumptions based on how Black women are portrayed in the media, where our bodies are hypersexualized, and our identities are flattened into narrow stereotypes.

What made this even more difficult was being told I didn't have the "stature" or "features" of the Black women they were familiar with—those they had seen on television or in music videos. As a result, I was often assumed to be mixed-race, or "mulatta," as if Blackness itself was confined to a single, exaggerated image.

The weight of these words people addressed me with depended on the context, the tone, and who was saying them. In some cases, older women or friendly locals would say *negrita* as a term of familiarity, much like they might say *flaca* (skinny girl) or guapa (pretty girl). But other times, it felt othering...like I was being reduced to my Blackness in a way that made me stand out even more. Unlike in the U.S., where racial terms like this carry a different weight, in Spain, these words were often used freely without much thought to how they might be received.

It was a strange dynamic to navigate. On one hand, I was constantly being noticed, sometimes with admiration or curiosity, and on the other, I had to process what it meant to be labeled in ways I wasn't entirely comfortable with.

Breaking Down Stereotypes

This experience highlighted a larger issue about how race is viewed in Spain, especially in regions with less exposure to diverse populations. The media's portrayal of Black women as either hypersexual beings or nothing at all created a distorted perception. My presence didn't fit neatly into these preconceived notions, and rather than embracing the diversity within Blackness, people struggled to categorize me in ways that were familiar to them.

However, it's important to note that this issue isn't unique to Spain. Stereotypes about Black women exist worldwide, often shaped by media and a lack of personal experiences. What I encountered was just a different manifestation of these global narratives.

Cultural Awareness and Growth

While some interactions were disheartening, they also sparked important conversations about race, identity, and representation. I took these moments as opportunities to challenge misconceptions and share a broader perspective of what it means to be a Black woman—complex, multifaceted, and far more than what's depicted in popular media.

Spain is a beautiful country with rich cultural diversity, but like anywhere, there is room for growth. The more we encourage dialogue, awareness, and education, the closer we come to breaking down harmful stereotypes and seeing people as individuals rather than representations of race or ethnicity.

Hair Styling For Black Women:

Finding a salon that knows how to handle afro-textured hair can be a challenge, especially outside of big cities. If you're in Madrid, head to the La Latina area. There, you'll find Dominican hair salons and African braiding shops that cater to our hair. If you're staying in a smaller region, consider getting a protective style before you leave the US, so you don't have to worry about hair care as much while abroad.

Climate

Since I've cleared the air on the racial climate let's get into the literal climate. The weather in Castilla y León? It's all over the place. I landed in April, and on my very first day, during the orientation and tour, it poured! I'm so glad I had an umbrella tucked away.

After that, it was chilly. My trench coat? It didn't stand a chance. I needed a real coat for a while. A sweater was a must from April to June. And when it did warm up, it got really warm. The sun in Spain feels like it's got something to prove. There were days when it was just in the 70s, but the sun made it feel much hotter. So, if you're heading to Castilla y León, do yourself a favor and pack for all seasons.

Oh, and whenever I traveled to Madrid, it was consistently warmer by almost 10 degrees, so be ready for that too!

Staying Connected

Let me just save you from the nightmare I went through: Do NOT, under any circumstances, try to use your U.S. phone plan while living in Europe for four months. Trust me, I've been there, done that, and got slapped with terrifying roaming and international fees. It was traumatizing, to say the least. But hey, at least my pain can be your gain!

Here's what you need to know:

First things first, if you're planning on staying abroad for a while, your best bet is to ditch the U.S. plan and get a local one. Seriously.

The good news? There are apps like Airalo, Holafly, and Nomad that make it super easy to stay connected without breaking the bank. Just make sure your phone is unlocked before you leave the States. Otherwise, you'll be out of luck.

Once I got that sorted, I switched to using WhatsApp as my go-to for all calls and messaging. It was a lifesaver. Spain is six hours ahead of New York, so catching my family at the right time meant waiting until I was done with dinner or people back home off work. For friends I made in Spain, we stayed in touch over Instagram, sharing updates on each other's lives.

Oh, and I can't forget about Google Translate! It was my BFF when I needed to get my point across in Spanish. Just talk right into the app, and boom, instant translation.

Staying connected with people in Spain was one thing, but keeping up with friends and family back in the U.S.? That was a whole different challenge. Social media helped. I could share my travels and experiences, and that was a way for everyone to see what was going on with me. But when it came to really staying in touch beyond the highlight reel, it wasn't always easy.

With Spain being six hours ahead, those time differences made catching up a struggle at times. I found myself staying up late just to squeeze in those real, deep conversations. I'd fit my calls into weekends or text constantly to keep everyone updated.

I learned to truly appreciate the people who made the effort to check in on me during my journey. The ones who were genuinely interested in my new life abroad.

Their curiosity and support meant the world to me, especially in moments when I felt far from home.

Full transparency, sometimes it felt like people back home couldn't really relate to what I was going through. When I shared the amazing things happening in Spain, I'd catch myself wondering if I sounded like I was bragging.

That was a tough line to walk... Trying to share my wins without feeling like I was overdoing it. I knew that people back home were still living their lives, and their lives didn't stop just because I was in another country having this amazing opportunity.

As a Black woman, I've noticed we don't always get the space to truly soak in our successes, to be proud of what we've achieved without feeling like we're being too much.

But looking back, I realize that staying connected physically, emotionally, and spiritually evolves as you do. As you grow and achieve new things, those connections will shift, and that's okay. It's part of the journey.

What to Do

Local and Tourist Advice

Tipping:

Unlike in the US, tipping isn't a big deal in Spain. It's not expected and certainly not necessary, but if you receive exceptional service, rounding up the bill is a simple and appreciated gesture. For instance, if your bill is €18.50, you might round it up to €20. But don't stress about it. No one's going to side-eye you if you don't tip.

Learn Basic Spanish Phrases:

If you're headed to bustling cities like Madrid or Barcelona, you'll find that many locals speak some English, especially in tourist hotspots. Trust me, learning a few basic Spanish phrases will go a long way. Even simple greetings and expressions can make interactions smoother and more pleasant.

If you're venturing into smaller regions like Castilla y León, though, it's a whole different story. English speakers are few and far between, so brushing up on your Spanish is crucial. And if you're like me and your Spanish isn't perfect, have a translator app handy. The locals appreciate the effort, even if you stumble through a few words.

The more I tried to speak Spanish, the more people appreciated it because Spaniards love to connect. I made an effort whenever I had the chance, and they respected that. But one thing about Spain, people will talk to you in full-on Spanish, even if they know you barely understand!

There were also days when trying to translate everything into English was exhausting. After a while, I realized that it was okay to just be a tourist sometimes, to take a break from trying so hard. Learning a language is a process, and some days, you just need to give yourself grace.

Download Your Maps:

Navigating through Spain's winding streets can be tricky, especially in older parts of the country where GPS signals might struggle. I recommend downloading your maps in advance using whatever app you prefer.

Google Maps, Apple Maps, Maps.me, you name it. This way, you can access your maps offline, so you're never lost, even when you can't find Wi-Fi or don't want to use up your data. Trust me, it's a lifesaver, especially when you're exploring a new city.

Bring an Adapter for Your Plug-In Items:

Spain operates on a different electrical system than the US. So, before you plug in your phone, laptop, or any other device, make sure you have a power adapter that works with European outlets. They use a 230V supply voltage and 50Hz, so your American gadgets need the right adapter to charge safely. You can grab a universal adapter online or at the airport, just don't forget it—nobody wants to be stuck with a dead phone on day one!

Invest in Travel Insurance:

Travel insurance is one of those things you don't think you need until you actually do. I'm talking about coverage that handles everything from lost luggage and trip cancellations to health emergencies. Some insurance plans even cover theft, so you can travel with peace of mind. You don't want to be caught off guard by unexpected situations, so it's worth the investment. Make sure the plan you choose covers all the essentials—better safe than sorry, right?

Watch Out for Pickpocketing:

Pickpocketing is real in tourist-heavy areas, so be alert, especially in places like Madrid's Gran Vía or Barcelona's Las Ramblas.

My go-to tip? A crossbody bag that zips closed and stays close to your body. It's harder for someone to snatch your stuff if your bag's secure and in sight. Avoid carrying valuables in your back pockets, and keep an eye on your belongings when you're in crowded spots or public transportation.

Let me give you some background on why I suggest limiting your hair styling if you're not in the main cities:

I had a curly sew-in. I messaged a stylist with a picture of my hair and asked very specific questions about whether she could do my hair properly. I only wanted a wash and set. After she assured me she could, I arrived for the appointment, and the experience was terrible.

She did wash my hair well, but she didn't condition it. That was something I made clear was essential for my curly sew-in. I tried to explain the order of steps for applying products, but she insisted her way was better. When it came time to blow-dry, she applied no products at all and tugged on my hair the whole time. It was honestly horrible, and I'm still traumatized.

And then, after all that, she had the audacity to say, *"You have an AFRO; these are not curls. I don't have the products for your hair…"* This was in Valladolid, Castilla y León, so trust me… don't make the same mistake I did. Come better prepared!

...

Explore Less-Visited Areas:

While cities like Madrid and Barcelona are amazing, don't sleep on the lesser-known regions of Spain. I might be a bit biased, but Castilla y León is an absolute gem. This region is steeped in history, with charming villages that feel like they're straight out of a storybook. It's a slower pace of life, and you'll see a side of Spain that's worlds away from the tourist hotspots. Whether you're wandering through medieval castles or sipping wine in a quiet plaza, it's worth taking the road less traveled.

Make Connections:

Moving to a new place can feel isolating, but don't worry—you're not alone. I found that joining Facebook and WhatsApp groups specifically for expats or travelers was a game-changer. I've met some incredible people who became friends, travel buddies, and even my support system while abroad. Social media is your friend here, so use it to your advantage! There are groups for everything: from expat communities to special interest groups where you can find people who share your hobbies.

Practice Your Spanish Everywhere

Speaking Spanish, even just a little bit, can make all the difference in your experience. I wasn't fluent, but I made it a point to use the Spanish I knew in everyday interactions. Whether it was ordering food, asking for directions, or just making small talk with locals, the effort was always appreciated. And honestly, it helped me build stronger connections with people. It's okay if you're not perfect. Most people will be patient and kind as long as you try. Plus, it's a great way to practice and improve your skills!

Some useful Facebook groups I joined during my time in Spain were:

- Move to Spain
- BWLA (Black Women Living Abroad)
- Barcelona Expats: International BCN
- Auxiliares de Conversación en Madrid (specific to English teachers)
- Digital Nomads Spain
- Friends in Barcelona
- Melanin Madrid (a great community for connecting)

To find the best groups for your city, simply search on Facebook for your destination and join the ones that resonate with you.

Many of these groups will have links to their WhatsApp chats where members share updates on local events, job opportunities, and community plans.

These groups are a fantastic resource for adjusting to life abroad whether you're connecting with seasoned expats or finding someone who's new to the experience like you.

Major Attractions

Ah, *Castilla y León*, the largest community in Spain. This region is so full of life and culture that I felt full just waking up here every day. From medieval cities to vineyards stretching across the landscape, it's a place that wraps you up in its history and beauty. It's steeped in cultural riches, with each town and city offering its own unique charm and story.

Cuéllar:

I have to talk about my home in Spain, first. **Cuéllar.** This village may be small, but it is bursting with history. Living here as a New Yorker felt like I had stepped into a different time. The Castillo de Cuéllar, a fortress dating back to the 10th century, watches over the village with its grand, medieval presence.

Cuéllar is famous for its medieval festivals and the annual bull running tradition. It's hard to describe the feeling of living in a place so different from the fast-paced, modern life I knew back in New York. Walking through the streets, surrounded by stone walls and centuries-old architecture, I found a peace and connection to history that was completely new to me. This village truly left its mark on my heart.

Salamanca:

The heartbeat of student life in Castilla y León. Home to one of the oldest universities in Europe, the University of Salamanca, this vibrant city is packed with youthful energy and history. Walking through its cobbled streets, you can feel the centuries of knowledge and passion that have passed through here. The Plaza Mayor is the perfect spot for people-watching, soaking up the sun, and getting lost in the hustle of students, tourists, and locals alike.

Segovia:

Segovia's iconic Roman aqueduct feels like something out of a dream. And it is. The aqueduct is a testament to Roman engineering. It towers over the city with such grace and precision.

Then there's the Alcázar of Segovia, the fairytale castle that actually inspired Disney's Cinderella Castle. You can literally walk through a Disney dream here. The views from the top of the castle are breathtaking. The whole city feels like stepping into another era, where the ancient and the charming meet perfectly. It's only about an hour outside of Madrid, which makes it a perfect day trip.

Valladolid:

If you're craving a little hustle and bustle, Valladolid is where it's at. A bustling city known for great shopping, Valladolid is a transportation hub and a perfect blend of old and new. There's something special about strolling through its streets, passing grand plazas and historical monuments, and then stepping into a chic modern café or boutique. The history here runs deep, especially as it was once the capital of Spain, so it's not just about shopping but soaking in the significance of the city's past.

Outside of the Castilla y Leon Region

Madrid:

Oh, Madrid... There's something electric about Spain's capital. It was exactly what I needed while living in Spain to remind me of home. It's just an easy hop from Valladolid or Segovia, and you can feel the city's pulse as soon as you arrive.

It's a city that never sleeps. The nightlife, endless shopping, world-class museums, and cozy cafes invite you to linger for hours. Every time I left my little village to spend a day in Madrid, I was reminded of how vibrant and exciting city life can be. It was a great balance.

Make sure to visit the Royal Palace or take a peaceful walk through Retiro Park, Madrid offers something for everyone.

Sample Itineraries

Most of my travels throughout Spain were on the weekends. The great thing about teaching for me was the schedule. At one point, I was off from Thursday until Sunday. Most of my trips were extremely tight on time but were so amazing!

Starting with **Barcelona**, my favorite city in Spain. Luckily for me, I was accompanied by a Barcelona local to show me the town, but if I were you, I'd highly recommend following this!

- **Paella Cooking Class**
  This was my first time attending a cooking class, but it was amazing, fun, and interactive. I booked through "the paella club." I did the "full menu experience" and paid €95. The ticket purchase included unlimited wine throughout the class, a 5-course dining experience, and lasted about 3 hours. Afterwards, you get to leave with a full recipe on how to make authentic Spanish paella. You are guided through every step of the cooking process in pairs of two.

- **Watch a soccer match**
  When Barcelona's biggest matches are on, like the El Clásico (FC Barcelona vs. Real Madrid),

the excitement spills out into the streets. Fans gather in public squares or streets around the city, particularly in areas like La Ramblas and Plaza Catalunya. During major matches, you'll often see people standing outside bars, glued to the screens from the street, chanting and celebrating together.

In the Barceloneta neighborhood, along the beach, fans often set up public viewing areas where they watch games on portable screens or TVs in outdoor spaces. It's a casual, laid-back environment with a mix of locals, tourists, and beachgoers all enjoying the match.

Another notable spot is Plaza de España, where during major tournaments like the World Cup or Euro Cup, massive outdoor screenings are sometimes organized, drawing a huge and diverse crowd. This is one of the best places to experience the energy of a live match surrounded by fellow fans from all walks of life.

Since Barcelona is an incredibly walkable city, I'd suggest doing all your heavy hitter tourist sights, if you are able to, in one day. Remember to purchase your tickets in advance.

Begin with Gaudi's works...

First**, Casa Batlló.** They're extremely amazing to see in person. You can tell he was extremely meticulous at what he did.

Next, I'd walk to the **Sagrada Familia**. The Sagrada Familia is why people visit Barcelona. It is the largest unfinished Catholic church in the world. I promise you can just stand on the outside for hours in amazement. It took my breath away. I honestly couldn't believe my eyes! And that's coming from a not-so-easily-impressed New Yorker.

4. Climb the **Bunkers El Carmel.** Panoramic views of Barcelona from Spanish Civil War bunkers. Once you arrive, there's about a 15-minute walk to the top.

5. Plan a day trip to **Montserrat.** This is the reason I fell in love with Barcelona. It has it all: the beach, the city, and mountains. Before you even get to the mountain, the views traveling there are amazing and steep. If you're afraid of heights don't look down!

Montserrat is a national park (now declared) that was invaded by Napoleon, home to the Montserrat Museum. There are vendors on Saturdays that sell honey, oil, and really really amazing cheese. This is where I fell in love with pesto cheese.

Getting There

Traveling from Barcelona's city center to Montserrat is pretty straightforward. The journey is a mix of metro and train, and the views along the way are stunning.

First, hop on the L1 metro line from central Barcelona, then transfer to the Montserrat Express train at Plaça Espanya. The train will take you straight to Montserrat, and from there, it's just a quick ride up the mountain via the cable car or funicular. The whole journey is smooth, and it's an easy escape from the city if you're craving a day in nature.

I highly recommend bringing a jacket or planning your visit early in the day because once nightfall hits, it gets extremely chilly up in Montserrat. The mountain air cools down fast, so it's better to be prepared, especially if you're spending a lot of time exploring or hiking.

Barcelona's Nightlife

One thing I'll say... I've never partied or seen parties like the ones I experienced in Barcelona. The nightlife here is on another level. When I say it's active, I mean it's ACTIVE.

Here are some tips to surviving Barcelona's nightlife scene:

It starts late. And I mean late. Think CP time, but multiply it by 10. Don't even think about getting ready before 1 AM. The first time I went out, I didn't start getting dressed until 3 AM, and I showed up to the club around 4 AM. Yes, you read that right.

Expect to party until the sun comes up. If you're looking to tap out early, Barcelona nightlife may not be for you. The party keeps going until morning, so be prepared for a long night.

Dress code is strict. This is not the place to show up casually. Dress to impress because clubs here expect a polished look.

It's cheaper to go earlier. If you're trying to save some euros, show up earlier in the night. The later it gets, the more you'll pay. Expect entrance fees ranging from 20 to 40 euros if you roll in late.

Want a section? It's surprisingly easy to get one. Most clubs just require you to purchase a hookah, which typically costs between 80-100 euros. So, if you and your friends want a place to chill, this is a good option.

Club Recommendations

When it comes to nightlife, here are a few spots that never disappoint:

- **Shoko** *(my personal favorite)* – A beachfront club that blends great music with a sleek, stylish vibe.
- **Jamboree** – If you're into live music and a mix of genres, this is the spot to hit. It's got a bit of everything.
- **Opium** – Known for its upscale, international crowd and incredible location right by the beach. Expect top DJs and a high-energy scene.

For Your Last Day

After all that partying, **a beach day** is the perfect way to unwind.

Here's my insider tip: *Skip Barceloneta*. It's crowded

and overrated. Instead, head to **Badalona**, which is much quieter, cuter, and has clearer water. It's the perfect hidden gem for a more relaxed vibe.

After you've soaked up the sun, make sure to grab a meal at **Made in Sicily.** Trust me, this is some of the best Italian food I've ever had—and I know my food!

Here's what you need to order:

- **Original Margherita Pizza:** Simple, fresh, and perfectly balanced.
- **Bavette alla Carbonara Trufada:** A decadent take on carbonara with truffle. You'll thank me later.
- **Pistachio Tiramisu:** This dessert will change your life. Creamy, nutty, and the perfect end to your meal.
- **Wine:** *Tareni Gillo* – Crisp, refreshing, and pairs perfectly with the meal.

Where to Stay in Barcelona

If you're wondering which neighborhoods to stay in, here are my top picks:

Barcelona

- **El Poblenou:** A charming area away from the city center's hustle and bustle, perfect for a laid-back experience.
- **Gràcia:** Known for its laid-back, residential feel. It's social, but still chill, with a great local vibe.
- **Eixample Izquierda:** Posh and polished. If you're into beautiful architecture and a stylish atmcsphere, this is your spot.
- **Sarrià-Sant Gervasi:** The most posh of them all. It's elegant, quiet, and ideal if you want to experience the more luxurious side of Barcelona.

Next Stop: Valencia, Spain

Valencia. A laid-back beach town that immediately gave me San Diego vibes. The pace here is slower, and the people are definitely more reserved compared to other parts of Spain. Honestly, I didn't feel like I needed to spend a ton of time here, but it's perfect for a weekend trip if you're coming from Madrid. It's a nice break from the intensity of city life, and the change of scenery is so refreshing.

Now, let's talk about **paella.** I know I've mentioned it before, but Valencia is the home of paella. If you ask any Spaniard, they'll tell you this is where you'll find the best in the country, straight from the source. I can confirm: it's worth the hype. This city is super chill, and it's the kind of place where you just want to lounge around and take it slow.

Here's what you should do while you're in Valencia:

- **Playa Cabanyal:** This beach is the perfect spot to hang out. There's a ton of food options along the strip, so you can grab a bite and just soak in the beach vibes. It's way more low-key than the crowded beaches in other cities.

- **Gelato at Veneta:** Okay, you have to try the gelato here. Veneta is hands-down the best spot. After a day of wandering around, nothing hits better than their creamy, dreamy gelato.

- **Ciutat de las Artes y Ciencias:** This spot is iconic, with its futuristic architecture. But if you're here in the summer, take it up a notch by kayaking or paddle boarding in front of the museum. It's such a cool way to experience the area. And don't skip the green gardens! They've got everything from flowers to towering trees. It's a little oasis right in the city.

- **Marina Beach Club:** If you're in the mood to party, this is where you need to be. They host Afrobeats parties, and the vibe is just right. You'll dance until the sun goes down.

- **Valencia Fallas Festival:** If you can, try to plan your trip around March so you can catch the Fallas festival. The whole city comes alive with bonfires, fireworks, and these massive sculptures that they end up burning at the end. It's wild and definitely something you won't forget.

Next Stop: Madrid

Ah, **Madrid**. The Spanish version of New York City. I swear, if you dropped me in the middle of Madrid without telling me where I was, I'd probably think I was back in NYC. The energy, the hustle, the endless things to do. It's all there, just with a Spanish twist.

Every time I visited Madrid, I shopped a lot. This city became my go-to spot for retail therapy. Most of my time was spent in **Sol**, where the streets are lined with every shop you can think of. From high street brands to small local boutiques, it's all within walking distance. If you're a Zara or Mango fan, be prepared to go wild. These Spanish brands always have better selections (and prices!) in Madrid than back home.

Now, if you're in Madrid on a Sunday, you have to check out **El Rastro**, the biggest flea market I've ever seen. And I've seen some big ones. This market has everything: fur coats, leather handbags, souvenirs, dresses, you name it. Most of the stalls sell for pretty cheap too, but make sure to bring cash because not everyone takes cards. El Rastro is located along **Plaza de Cascorro** and **Ribera de Curtidores**, and it's a whole vibe, so plan to spend some time wandering around.

If you're looking for more high-end shopping, head to Serrano in the Salamanca district. This is Madrid's luxury shopping area, where you'll find all the big-name designers like Loewe, Chanel, and Louis Vuitton. Even if you're just window shopping, it's a beautiful area to walk through, with wide tree-lined streets and elegant storefronts.

For a more unique shopping experience, **Embajadores** was my favorite area. It's filled with cute, quirky shops where you can find one-of-a-kind pieces, from handmade jewelry to vintage clothes. This neighborhood has a more laid-back, artsy vibe, and it's perfect if you're hunting for something different from the usual commercial spots.

Brunch and Jazz in Madrid

If you're looking for a good brunch spot, **Botania** is the place to go. It's set in a beautiful, lush green space that makes you feel like you've escaped the city. The food is just as impressive as the décor. Think fresh juices, eggs benedict, and the fluffiest pancakes. It's the perfect spot to recharge after a morning of shopping or sightseeing.

For something a little different, if you're a jazz fan (or just looking for a cool, chill night out), you have to check out **Café El Despertar**. This intimate spot in Lavapiés offers live jazz performances that are some of the best I've heard. The vibe is so relaxed, and it feels like you've stumbled upon a hidden gem. Definitely stop by if you want to wind down your evening with good music.

Street Performers & Tango Shows in Madrid

One thing you absolutely can't miss while wandering around Madrid is the street performers. The city is full of life, and you'll find some of the most talented performers scattered throughout the main squares and parks. Be sure to check out **Plaza Mayor** and **Puerta del Sol**—these areas are always buzzing with musicians, dancers, and even living statues. It's like free entertainment on every corner. I spent hours just strolling through these spots, watching flamenco guitarists and dancers bring so much energy to the streets.

Another place to catch some unique performances is **Parque del Retiro**, especially on weekends. The park is full of buskers, magicians, and artists, all adding to

the vibrant atmosphere. Grab a snack from a nearby vendor, find a bench, and just enjoy the show.

Where to Find Tango Shows:

If you're looking to experience something a little more intimate and sultry, I highly recommend checking out a tango show while you're in Madrid. You can find some amazing tango performances at **El Café de Chinitas**, a charming venue that hosts traditional Spanish shows. While they're known for flamenco, they often incorporate tango into their performances, and the ambiance is perfect for a more refined night out.

For a more dedicated tango experience, visit **Casa Patas**. It's one of Madrid's most iconic spots for live dance performances, and you'll find a mix of flamenco and tango that will leave you absolutely mesmerized. The dancers here are incredibly passionate, and the live music adds an extra layer of magic to the performance. It's a beautiful way to experience some of Spain's rich dance culture.

Madrid's Nightlife

Now, if you're looking to experience Madrid's famous nightlife, head over to the **Alberto Alcocer Strip**. This area is packed with clubs, and the party doesn't stop until the early hours of the morning. Some of the most popular clubs along the strip include Teatro Kapital,

Opium Madrid, Joy Eslava, and Zsongo.

Zsongo is a must-visit if you're into Afrobeat and reggaeton. It has a unique, lively atmosphere that keeps the crowd dancing all night. Whether you're into electronic music, reggaeton, or hip-hop, you'll find something to suit your vibe here. Just make sure to dress to impress because the nightlife in Madrid is as stylish as it is lively.

And after all that dancing, if you're like me and love a good cocktail, you've got to try an espresso martini at **Rambal** in Lavapiés. I'm not exaggerating when I say it's the best espresso martini I've ever had. **Lavapiés** is also an amazing area to explore—vibrant, diverse, and full of life.

Returning Home: Navigating the Readjustment

What I didn't expect was the reverse culture shock that hit me upon returning to the U.S. After being away—removed from what I call the overstimulation of life in America as a Black woman—coming back felt overwhelming. Let's be real: the current climate in the U.S. isn't exactly something to look forward to. If it were, why are so many people trying to leave?

Honestly, I'd highly recommend therapy. Even with a strong support system, you need someone who truly understands what you're experiencing. For me, being abroad was the first time I ever felt like my true self. **I felt empowered.**

I was still Black, but not in America.

I've always taken pride in my Blackness, but in the U.S., there are so many limiting factors. I didn't feel that in Spain. The food was better, life was more active, I was more sociable, and the food was clean. People engaged with each other and were genuinely interested in your life. They wanted to know you, not just what you could do for them. Things I didn't often experience back in the U.S.

Being the first in my family to move abroad, I had no guide to prepare me for what it would be like to return. Months later, I'm still adjusting. And to be honest? I've been trying to go back ever since I landed.

No one talks about the high you feel while abroad—the freedom, the adventure, the sense of possibility—and the harsh reality that sets in once you return. The crash is real. The sadness is real. People around me don't always understand why the transition has been so hard, but the truth is, my life felt completely different over there.

I got to really live...

In Spain, there was no pressure to always be on the go. People lived their lives without the obsession of work. They took time to connect, to enjoy. But here in the U.S., it's all about the grind. I got to truly live in Spain, and that's a feeling I don't want to lose.

One thing I've learned about adjusting back? **Create routines.** Find your happy place. Pick a café, a park, a hobby to keep you grounded.

After waking up every day in awe of the beauty around me in Spain, it was tough to return to a world of highways and endless errands. Now, I make a point to look for beauty in the little things.

Lately, that's meant sitting on a bench and people-watching, staring up at the moon, and catching the sunset. Coming home in the fall, I've literally fallen in love with the leaves changing color all over again. Small moments like these bring me peace.

I'm also focusing on strengthening my relationships with the people who supported me while I was away and distancing myself from anything or anyone that doesn't bring me joy.

Spain made me fall in love with things I never expected to enjoy. But just because I'm not there doesn't mean I can't still embrace them. For example, Spain made me love beer—like, really love it. With this newfound appreciation, it opened the door for me to enjoy cider and beer tastings at breweries and orchards in New York during the fall.

Being back home, I've learned to appreciate the simple pleasures—the laughter I share with people, the ease and convenience of life here, and yes, even being able to wear sweats without judgment. It's the little comforts that are keeping me grounded.

I can also savor good ol' American food: pizza, French fries, chicken wings, bodega sandwiches, and burgers. Shopping at Trader Joe's again, as it was one of the things I loved before leaving the U.S. I've fallen in love with these comforts all over again.

This adventure was just one chapter of my journey, but it changed me. It pushed me to see more, to dream bigger, and most importantly, to see myself more clearly. I am full because I got to experience it with my own eyes. We only get one life, and in this one, I'm choosing to chase my wildest dreams. Maybe in the next, I'll play it safe—who knows?

So yes, I'd love to go back, and one day I will. This experience has taught me something much more profound: *to seek out God's beauty in everything, because He is everywhere.* I just have to pay attention...

Alexa play "Overjoyed"
by Stevie Wonder

Who's Behind This Guide?

Wow! who knew I'd be writing my own bio for a story? Actually, I did know, but I didn't think it would happen this soon. It's surreal to look back and see how stepping outside of my comfort zone didn't just broaden my horizons. It redefined how I see myself.

When I moved to Spain, I thought I was going for the adventure, the teaching, and the chance to travel. And while I embraced all of that, I didn't expect the journey to open my eyes to something far greater. Leaving behind everything familiar forced me to shed the expectations I had of myself and discover who I truly was.

Yes, I was a foreigner. Immersed in a new culture, navigating a different language, and standing out in ways I hadn't before... But it was in those moments of unfamiliarity that I found clarity. Spain didn't just give me stories to tell. It gave me the space to grow, to connect with myself beyond the roles and norms I had known

Losing my mom at five taught me a truth that's shaped my life: time is fleeting, and nothing is promised. It pushed me to rely on spirit and to trust in something bigger than myself. That belief has been my foundation—guiding me through every obstacle and reminding me that life doesn't get easier. Instead, you grow stronger in faith, in resilience, and in purpose. And in that growth, you find meaning.

This guide isn't just about navigating life in Spain. It's about stepping boldly into the unknown and discovering the beauty that comes from taking that leap.

So, who's behind this guide?

Someone who refuses to fit neatly into any box. I'm serious, but still a kid at heart. Soft-spoken yet fearlessly opinionated. Sensitive yet tough. Sassy yet sweet. So different, yet able to adapt and thrive anywhere. I'm dependable, thoughtful, and constantly evolving. The list could go on—and it will—because I believe in living a life without limits.

For now, I'll be the one with the faith of a mustard seed, who didn't need to know every detail of the blueprint but trusted the plan was already written.

-Kamryn Niane Kinlow
IG:@travelwithkamrynk | TikTok:@kryptoniteblackbykam

Keep up with Kamryn

www.travelingblackwomen.com